THE DINGLE PENINSULA

30 WALKS AND SCRAMBLES

THE DINGLE PENINSULA
30 WALKS AND SCRAMBLES

Barry Keane

THE COLLINS PRESS

To Louise

Published by The Collins Press, Carey's Lane, The Huguenot Quarter, Cork 1997

British Library Cataloguing in Publication data.

Printed in Ireland by Colour Books Ltd., Dublin

Jacket design by Upper Case Ltd., Cornmarket Street, Cork

ISBN: 1-898256-28-4

ACKNOWLEDGEMENTS

This book doesn't belong to anybody in particular, but all the people who have climbed, walked and crawled these the past twenty years. Nobody is sure who completed all these routes first (most likely a farmer out looking for sheep in his Sunday best, wellies, cap and stick). The local clubs in Tralee, Dingle, UCC, Killarney, and Cork also share some of the blame.

My mountaineering career began on Mangerton with 78 other first year students from Cólaiste an Spioraid Naoimh in Cork. Having been literally blown off the summit of Stoompa and then forced to walk in the rain all the way into Killarney, it was a wonder that any of us went back. The school club is still going strong and I wish it the best in the future.

The main contributors to the guide, besides myself, are in no particular order: Con O'Sullivan, Vince Hargy, Des O'Brien, Annemarie and Kate Pollock, John Hawe, Trish McEneanny, James O'Reilly, Willie Rattray, Sinead Daly, Finbarr Desmond, Brian (Geology) Jones, Fiona O'Sullivan, Brian Gebruers, Donnacha Nelan, Tim Cotter, and Mark O'Gorman. All the members of the UCC Mountaineers for their help and assistance in doing and redoing the routes deserve special thanks.

I would also like to thank The Collins Press for having faith, infinite patience and for putting

some form to my ramblings; Joe Cronin for allowing us to use the excellent photo that adorns the
front cover; and Henry O'Keeffe who proof-read
the original text and did a fine job on the ideas
front deserves a special thank you.

Finally I would like to thank my parents for
allowing me out on the mountains from the age of
13, a gift that will always be impossible to repay.
Thanks also to Louise for putting up with it all.

CONTENTS

SECTION I   THE SLIABH MISH

SECTION II   STRADBALLY

SECTION III   BRANDON

SECTION IV   MOUNT EAGLE , AND THE
BLASKETS

1. ACCOMMODATION
Contact Bord Fáilte (the Irish Tourist Board) for anything from five-star hotels to Bed and Breakfasts. The independent hostels are inexpensive and excellent places to stay and are dotted all over the peninsula. Many are into the climbing scene and are great sources of information about the area.

2. MAPS
1:50,000 O.S. maps cover the whole area. 70 and 71 cover Dingle. The sketch maps in the book are schematic diagrams, and are not designed to be a substitute for the Ordnance Survey Maps. See also **Safety.**

3. ACCESS
Access is usually not a problem, but specific problems do arise from time to time. *Irish Mountain Log* usually gives you notice of any access problems but these are short-lived at best. Traditionally, climbers, hillwalkers and farmers have always got on. Ask permission if in doubt and there should be no problem. If you do meet a farmer on the hill, it is courteous and usual to stop for a chat.

4. GRADINGS
It is always very difficult to grade scrambles and what I find hard or easy may be different to others. The grades in the guide are based on personal

experience and the views of mountaineers who have either done the routes with me or followed my suggestions as to which climb is where.

Hillwalk 1: Easy half-day walks with no problems other than very minor navigational ones.

Hillwalk 2: Longer walks with no rough ground, or a few navigational problems.

Hillwalk 3: Longer walks which require reasonable mountain knowledge, and navigation skills required. Usually the ground will be rough underfoot and some steep slopes will be encountered.

Hillwalk 4: Long day walks. Rough, tough and with good mountain skills required, especially in misty conditions.

Hillwalk 5: Multi-day walks usually along the peninsula. For the committed backpacker or those on a couple of days holiday.

Scramble 1: Easy scrambles on hillwalks, most of which can be avoided. Hands would not normally be required except for the occasional balancing act.

Scramble 2: More scrambling, slightly steeper with less options to avoid everything.

Scramble 3: More committing but easy to retreat either left or right to easier ground. Vegetation or loose rock may be a problem. The odd easy rockclimbing move will present itself.

Scramble 4: Harder climbs with little or no escape routes and the odd moderate rockclimbing move.

Loose rock and vegetation a problem.

Scramble 5: Committing climbs, very exposed or in gullies. Moves up to difficult will occur.

Scramble 6/Rock 1: Sustained, steep, wet, loose and hard, usually buttresses with the occasional very difficult move. Rope advisable.

Scramble 7/Rock 2: Mainly rockclimbing routes which are technically challenging with moves from very difficult to severe and a rope is more than advisable.

NB. Add one grade if the rock is wet. As the rock is loose it is better to treat it with a bit of care. Over the years we have found it better to push up on the holds rather than tugging them to see if they are solid.

5.
a. Distances and Timings of Walks
All distances are in metres (m) or kilometres (km) as appropriate, and the total distance is given from start to finish of the day. The scrambles obviously only take up a small part of the total day out.

b. Heights
All heights are given in metres and the height gain is the total ascent for the day, give or take a few metres.

c. Time

This is a rough guide based on 15 minutes per kilometre and 3 minutes per 30 metres which has served me well over the years in the south-west. However, rests are not included, so these should also be taken into account. Fit groups will have no bother in beating the guidebook time, but they might not enjoy the view.

6. Route Number and Name

Each route is numbered and given a name. In many cases these names will not be known to some climbers as different names are used for many places in the Kerry and West Cork hills. As Dingle is a Gaeltacht area, the names tend to drift between Irish and English so many peaks may not be instantly recognisable to visitors. Fortunately, the new maps tend to have both the Irish and English names so there are no huge problems. However to give you a flavour of how things work, Drom na Muice (Route 22) means The Pigs Back, while its neighbour Garranceol (Route 21) means The Garden of Music.

7. Route Description

I have tried to include the main features of all routes, be they walks or scrambles, but what I find significant may not be to the person on the route. However, as a general rule, all scrambles go straight up from the bottom of the route with little traversing from left to right. I must emphasise that it is up to the person climbing the route to use their common sense. All gully routes stay in the gully unless otherwise mentioned.

8. SAFETY

Let's be blunt, people get killed in the mountains. Anyone going into the Irish hills at any time must be in the company of someone who can navigate, or can navigate themselves. This is not an optional extra. No guidebook can hope to get you up and down a mountain route in safety – it can only suggest options and possibilites. After that you are entirely on your own.

You must also have the correct equipment: rain gear, food, spare clothing a first-aid kit and rudimentary bivouac equipment are also essential items.

The extreme changability of the weather means that you should always have a good idea of the weather forecast, and be willing to turn back if the weather is too bad.

A basic knowledge of first-aid is also something that is needed as help can be many hours away, and it may well be up to you to keep someone alive.

An understanding of winter climbing when snow lies on the hills is also a vital requirement. Some of the most horrible accidents occur to people who slipped on a patch of snow, and were not able to stop themselves from falling. Scramblers should have a knowledge of basic rope techniques and enough rock climbing knowledge to belay someone safely up or down a route.

Remember there are few, if any tracks in the Irish hills, and very few people so you are on your own most of the time. This puts a greater responsiblity on the mountaineer to be self-sufficent, but also allows you much greater freedom. All of this can be learnt by osmosis in your local mountaineering or hillwalking club, but once you have the basics you can discover the hills for yourself.

9. EQUIPMENT

The essential item of equipment for a scrambler is a pair of 3 season mountaineering boots with at least a three-quarter shank. For hillwalking you can purchase an ordinary pair of walking boots with good waterproofing, and good protection for the ankle. After that you will need raingear, a rope, some slings, a minimal amount of rock climbing equipment, map compass, rescue equipment, and a rucksack narrow enough to fit your back.

10. RESCUE

The Kerry Mountain Rescue team cover the Dingle Peninsula. Call the Gardaí if you have a problem, and they will alert the rescue services for you.

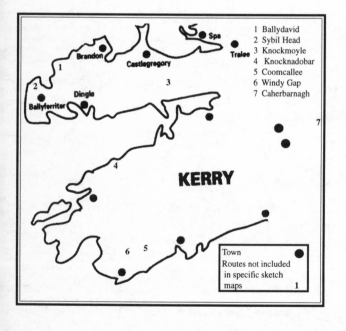

1 Ballydavid
2 Sybil Head
3 Knockmoyle
4 Knocknadobar
5 Coomcallee
6 Windy Gap
7 Caherbarnagh

KERRY

Town
Routes not included
in specific sketch
maps

16

ROUTE 1

Mountain Group:	The Sliabh Mish
Route Name:	The Glanbrack Horseshoe
Distance from start to finish:	13km
Height Gain:	891m
Average time from start to finish:	5–6 hrs
Starting Grid Reference:	794118
Grade:	Hillwalk 3
Map:	1
O.S. map 1:50,000:	71

1. This is a fine tour including Baurtregaum, the highest peak in the Sliabh Mish hills at 851m. The views are superb on the narrowest part of the Dingle peninsula. Start at the holiday village (794118) on the straight road between Blennerville and Camp, about 2.5km from Blennerville. Do not go up the road into the holiday village, but the one just to the east of it. Follow this straight up until it turns sharp right. A track goes straight on and over a gate onto the mountainside. Continue uphill to Knockauncorragh 567m. Continue along the broad ridge to spot 597m, which is very difficult to find in mist. Head west northwest over Glanbrack Mountain, an insignificant hump on the ridge, and then west southwest to Baurtregaum. Spot 677m is actually marked by a cairn,

unlike Glanbrack Mountain. The ground looks like a massive raised beach and is caused by the conglomerate breaking down. The last 200m to the summit are quite steep but the 851m summit is quickly reached. The trig. station is set among a whole series of stone shelters of uncertain age and is unmistakable. Descend east northeast to spot 819m and then down the long northeast ridge to point 603m, a little rise on the ridge. Cross the Curraheen river at a footbridge on the Dingle Way by a small reservoir (783786) and follow the Dingle Way back to your start point.

ROUTE 2

Mountain Group:	The Sliabh Mish
Route Name:	Curraheen Glen
Distance from start to finish:	10km
Height Gain:	654m
Average time from start to finish:	3.5–4.5 hrs
Starting Grid Reference:	794118
Grade:	Scramble 1
Map:	1
O.S. map 1:50,000:	71

2. Instead of going up Knockauncorragh on the Glanbrack Horseshoe, the Curraheen Glen (782 097) offers a good alternative. Park as for route one (794118), and head into the glen. A prominent stream coming in from your left should be crossed and heading south southwest you will come to the steep ground of the spur called Gowlane. Climbing the spur is quite easy with a few scrambly options and one or two steps. However, the fun ends quickly and you trudge up the easy ground onto the summit of Glanbrack Mountain. This is a nice introduction to scrambling.

ROUTE 3

Mountain Group:	The Sliabh Mish
Route Name:	Derrymore Glen
Distance from start to finish:	10.5km
Height Gain:	855m
Average time from start to finish:	4–5 hrs
Starting Grid Reference:	743107
Grade:	Scramble 1 or 2
Map:	1
O.S. map 1:50,000:	71

3. After Derrymore Bridge take either of the two turns to your left. The second one is better. Park by the shed of turf (743107) at the end of the boreen. Ask permission if in doubt, and then follow the track south, and then immediately west out onto the mountain by some sheep pens. Follow the river into the Glen. The first fall of water can be quite tricky and it can be avoided by traversing around to the right (facing south). A path runs along the west bank of the stream past some old workings and to Derrymore lake which still has its old dam almost intact. Pick a line on the back wall of the coum and head up to the col between Baurtregaum and Caherconree. This can be tricky when wet. You can go either to Baurtregaum or Caherconree as the fancy takes you.

ROUTE 4

Mountain Group:	The Sliabh Mish
Route Name:	Caherconree Fort
Distance from start to finish:	5km
Height Gain:	585m
Average time from start to finish:	2.5–3.5 hrs
Starting Grid Reference:	717057
Grade:	Hillwalk 2
Map:	1
O.S. map 1:50,000:	71

4. From Camp village take the road south at Ashe's pub and head uphill to the col between Caherbla and Knockbrack where a line of red and white poles lead uphill from just under the summit of the col at (717057). A sign here gives you the bones of the Caherconree story and Sean O'Sullivan's *Southwest Walks* will give you full details. Anyway it is a fine example of a promontory fort and is worth a visit on its own. The red and white poles interspersed with fence poles lead over very boggy ground to a small col under the fort. From the col head north uphill to the fort. Head northeast to the summit of Caherconree. Descend the way you came.

ROUTE 5

Mountain Group:	The Sliabh Mish
Route Name:	Derrymore Horseshoe
Distance from start to finish:	11.25km
Height Gain:	1000m
Average time from start to finish:	4.5–5.5 hrs
Starting Grid Reference:	755113
Grade:	Hillwalk 3
Map:	1
O.S. map 1:50,000:	71

5. This is an excellent day out encompassing the four highest hills in the Sliabh Mish. Start at Derryquay National School, where there is parking on both sides of the road (755113). Hop over the back wall weaving your way through gorse bushes on sheep tracks to the Dingle Way. Head up the steep slog to Scragg, a spot height of 657m, at the start of the long ridge to Baurtregaum. Geologically you should come across red jaspar which is strikingly brighter than the predominant sandstone. The ridge steepens, and joins the northeast ridge at point 819m. A short walk will bring you to the summit of Baurtregaum (851m). This section can be extremely windy due to the wind roaring up the cliff to your left. However, it is only a short section and can be avoided by dropping

under the ridge line on the right hand side. Descend west southwest to the narrow col between Baurtregaum, and Caherconree and then push steeply up to the summit of Caherconree. The ground to your left falls 200m down a cliff so care is needed in this section. Continue from the summit cairn north to Gearhane. Then descend steeply northeast back to the Derrymore river and then back to the school via the Dingle Way.

Route 6

Mountain Group:	The Sliabh Mish
Route Name:	Sliabh Mish Ridge
Distance from start to finish:	20km
Height Gain:	677m
Average time from start to finish:	6–7 hrs
Starting Grid Reference:	835080
Grade:	Hillwalk 3
Map:	1
O.S. map 1:50,000:	71

6. A good day out can be had by parking you car on the col (835080) between Knocknawaddra and Knockmoyle. In many ways this is one of the more bizarre walks in the Kerry hills. It is in no way difficult but there is so much human iron-mongery lying around it looks like some enormous sculpture park. Having parked your car, head west on the track to the forest of communications towers. Follow the ridge line along the top of the military firing range and after a while you will be joined by a line of old telephone poles coming in from the north by the side of a track. This will lead to an old communications tower which is known locally as the Iron Man. It is well worth a visit on its own. Continue northwest from the Iron Man skirting a gentle glen on your left, and ascend steeply on to the flat summit of

Knockauncorragh. From the cairn head south southwest onto the main ridge and head west over boggy ground to the 'summit' of Glanbrack mountain. Don't hold your breath looking for it. Continue west and up steeply to the summit of Baurtregaum with about ten old shelters to keep the trig. point company. Return the way you came.

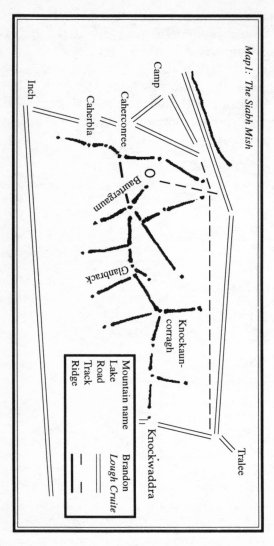

Map 1: The Siabh Mish

Tralee

Knockwaddra

Knockaun-corragh

Glanbrack

Baurtregaum

Caherbla

Caherconree

Camp

Inch

Mountain name	Brandon
Lake	*Lough Cruite*
Road	
Track	
Ridge	

26

Section II Stradbally
Route 7

Mountain Group:	Stradbally
Route Name:	Stradbally Mountain
Distance from start to finish:	10.5km
Height Gain:	984m
Average time from start to finish:	4.5–5.5 hrs
Starting Grid Reference:	627118
Grade:	Hillwalk 3
Map:	2
O.S. map 1:50,000:	70/71

7. One of the most neglected hills in all of Kerry must be Stradbally Mountain. On my visits to the area I have never met anyone. The ground is not particularly difficult and the views are excellent which makes it an enjoyable day out for anyone staying in the area. I would suggest leaving one car at the turn (627118) for Castlegregory at the grotto and another at the base of the track leading up to Scraggane (548107). Head west along the main road and take the next turn on your left. Follow this to the base of the east ridge of Stradbally Mountain, and follow this to the summit. According to some maps the wood on the northside goes all the way to the summit. It doesn't. Head southwest to the col and then up onto Beenoskee (826m), the highest peak in the area. Descend

northwest to An Com Bán along the wide ridge. A detour to Binn an Tuair where the view into the U-shaped Glenahoo valley is spectacular, is not only recommended, but is one of the finest hidden splendours in Kerry. Go north from here across the boggy ground to Ballyduff. If you have only one car you should descend from the summit of Beenoskee around Lough Acummeen down to the road at Stradbally and a pint in Tomasin's pub. A private hostel across the road can be booked in the pub.

ROUTE 8

Mountain Group:	Stradbally
Route Name:	Glenahoo
Distance from start to finish:	10km
Height Gain:	786m
Average time from start to finish:	4–5 hrs
Starting Grid Reference:	545010
Grade:	Hillwalk 3
Map:	2
O.S. map 1:50,000:	70

8. Park your car in Ballyduff (545010) and walk up the old road south into Glenahoo. This superb U-shaped valley is objective enough for a day out, but continue to the back wall which brings you to about 350m. This will bring you up by the left side of the waterfall which is very pleasant and then across the stream above it, out onto the bog. Turn left uphill to the summit of Beenoskee, a bit of a slog which steepens towards the top. Then descend northwest to the flat ground. Continue along to An Com Bán and back down to Ballyduff.

ROUTE 9

Mountain Group:	Stradbally
Route Name:	Glanteenassig Horseshoe
Distance from start to finish:	14km
Height Gain:	925m
Average time from start to finish:	5–6 hrs
Starting Grid Reference:	600078
Grade:	Hillwalk 3
Map:	2
O.S. map 1:50,000:	70/71

9. This is a long walk, which is well worth the effort. Drive to Araglen Forest Park (600078). Climb steeply to Doon 350m. Follow the level and boggy ridge south then southwest to spot 552m giving great views south over Anascaul. Head west to Dromavalla Mountain which has a burial mound on the summit. This is named on the old map but not on the new one. A line of standing stones lead away from the summit to the cliff edge above the glen. Then cross the boggy ground and up to Beenoskee, and then eastwards to Stradbally. From here it's down east until the ridge ends above Lough Araglen. Head south downhill to the track and forest park.

Route 10

Mountain Group:	Stradbally
Route Name:	Glanteenassig
Distance from start to finish:	8km
Height Gain:	588m
Average time from start to finish:	3–4 hrs
Starting Grid Reference:	600078
Grade:	Scramble 1 or 3
Map:	2
O.S. map 1:50,000:	70/71

10. The dubious benefit of planting acid conifers on acid bog is exciting much interest in Ireland at present. However Coillte, the Irish Forestry Commission, are very reasonable towards mountaineers tramping through the trails in their woods. Having parked sensibly at Lough Caum (600078), head west to the base of the cliffs. A ramp line will lead under a slab and up onto the south ridge of Stradbally mountain. The cliff offers a couple of routes outside the range of the guide, but you can also drift more north of the cliff to head up to the summit of the mountain. Descend down the east ridge to your car.

The back to back coums of Anascaul, and Glenahoo effectivly divide the Stradbally hills from those to the west. These tend to be lower than their eastern counterparts, and from the south are a very easy prospect. The northern escarpment is more difficult, but still not a huge problem as there are many ridges poking down from the summit. A visit to Tom Crean's South Pole Inn in Anascaul is an absolute must for any visitor to the area.

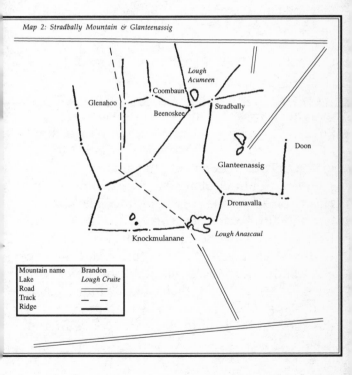

Map 2: *Stradbally Mountain & Glanteenassig*

Lough Acumeen

Coombaun

Glenahoo

Beenoskee

Stradbally

Doon

Glanteenassig

Dromavalla

Knockmulanane

Lough Anascaul

Mountain name	Brandon
Lake	*Lough Cruite*
Road	
Track	– – –
Ridge	

33

Route 11

Mountain Group:	Anascaul
Route Name:	Anascaul Horseshoe
Distance from start to finish:	10km
Height Gain:	800m
Average time from start to finish:	4–5 hrs
Starting Grid Reference:	583053
Grade:	Hillwalk 3
Map:	3
O.S. map 1:50,000:	70

11. Anascaul is a nice glen very much associated with the Fianna (Ireland's ancient warriors). Park your car at the carpark beside Lough Anascaul (583053). Ascend the easy slope to Cnoc Mhaoilionáin (595m) making sure to avoid the cliffs on your left. Continue along the ridge to point 641m. Head north over the bog past a little lake on your left and turn east once you hit the green road heading from Anascaul to Glenahoo. Continue until you are above the cliffs into Glanteenassig and admire the view. South then and up to Dromavalla Mountain with its burial mound and standing stones. From here pick a path through the gorse to the road in Anascaul glen and your car.

ROUTE 12

Mountain Group:	Anascaul
Route Name:	Carrigblaher
Distance from start to finish:	3km
Height Gain:	515m
Average time from start to finish:	2–3 hrs
Starting Grid Reference:	575050
Grade:	Scramble 1
Map:	3
O.S. map 1:50,000:	70

12. The Carrighblaher cliffs which guard the northern side of Cnoc Mhaoilionáin offer a couple of nice scrambles. The most obvious is the gully in the centre of the face. This is quite easy and is occasionally wet. Follow the green road by the side of the lake and inspect the cliffs. The gully is more than obvious. Climb it directly with some loose rock, a couple of little steps, and lots of grass. At the top of the gully go right to the summit.

ROUTE 13

Mountain Group:	Anascaul
Route Name:	Beenbo to Slievanea
Distance from start to finish:	16km (6km on road)
Height Gain:	900m
Average time from start to finish:	5.5–6.5 hrs
Starting Grid Reference:	541103
Grade:	Hillwalk 4
Map:	3
O.S. map 1:50,000:	70

13. Park at Ballyduff and at the crossroads go south. At the next junction go left and then strike out onto the open hillside. Head up the pleasant ridge to Beenbo. Head west to Slievenagower and then wander over the boggy and flat ground to the main ridge around Windy Gap above the many little lakes around here. Follow the ridge west, then northwest, to Slievanea, and descend west over An Crapán Mór to the track that leads back around to the Connor Pass. From here it is a 5km walk downhill to your car. There is a new track on the west side of Beenbo but this takes the fun out of it!

ROUTE 14

Mountain Group:	Anascaul
Route Name:	Slievanea Buttress
Distance from start to finish:	0.5km
Height Gain:	263m
Average time from start to finish:	1–1.5 hrs
Starting Grid Reference:	503062
Grade:	Scramble 3 or 5
Map:	3
O.S. map 1:50,000:	70

14. A sharp bend on the road to the Connor Pass from Castlegregory is where to park your car (503062) for this scramble. A number of picnic tables and litter bins make this a pleasant spot to have lunch. Follow the path by the stream gushing out of Lough Doon and you will come to the lake in short order. On the west side of the lake an excellent scramble with a few 10m rock steps will lead to the summit of Slievanea. It can be quite wet at times and a rope would not be a bad idea, just in case.

Brandon mountain is one of my own personal favourites. The gentle western side provides easy routes on to one of the highest mountains in Ireland, and it is a must for anyone staying in the area. At its foot Dingle town, (the home of Fungie the dolphin) is one of the finest towns in Ireland for the craic. On the western side of the mountain Killmacader church, Gallurus Oratory, and the Stone Age dwellings on the west side of Smerwick harbour add to the facination of the area. As this is also one of the last areas where Irish is spoken as an every day language the rich cultural heritage of the area practically leaks from the hills. There are few more beautiful spots than Dingle late in the autumn with the fuschia in bloom. The contrast with the eastern side of the mountain couldn't be greater. The savagery of the Paternoster glen is truly awful in the best sense of the word, with its steep walls and sharp ridges. The view out over the massive sand tombolo of Castlegregory is an enormous contrast to the glaciation of this side of the mountain. Unfortunately though, Brandon tends to attract whatever cloud there is around, so you may not be able to see a whole lot.

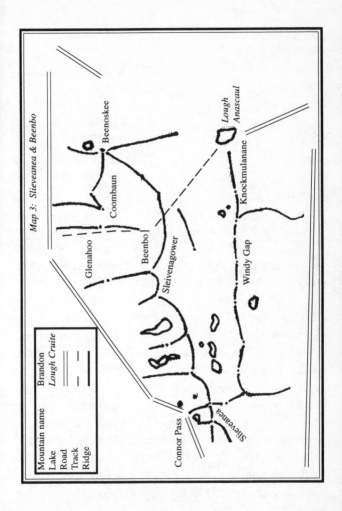

Map 3: Slieveanea & Beenbo

Mountain name: Brandon
Lake: Lough Cruite
Road
Track
Ridge

Beenoskee
Coombaun
Glenahoo
Beenbo
Sleivengower
Lough Anascaul
Knockmulanane
Windy Gap
Connor Pass
Slieveanea

39

ROUTE 15

Mountain Group:	Brandon
Route Name:	Ballysitteragh
Distance from start to finish:	17km (6km on road)
Height Gain:	813m
Average time from start to finish:	5.5–6.5 hrs
Starting Grid Reference:	440025
Grade:	Hillwalk 4
Map:	4
O.S. map 1:50,000:	70

15. Dingle town nestles at the foot of the Brandon massif. You can literally walk out your front door on to the open mountainside. Take the road north out of Dingle past the Hospital, and just before the Fire Station (440025). About 100m up this, take a lane to your right onto the open mountain. Follow the easy ridge which steepens as it approaches Beenbrack. The view is excellent from the summit. Head northwest towards Ballysitteragh. Either head west along the ridge down to the school-house for a short walk or drop down steeply to the col under Gearhane. Contour around for a few moments peace at Lough na mBan before contouring west to follow the ridge down to Ballinloghlig. It is a bit of a slog along the road to Dingle from here but the views usually tend to be pleasant.

ROUTE 16

Mountain Group:	Brandon
Route Name:	The Saint's Road
Distance from start to finish:	10km
Height Gain:	952m
Average time from start to finish:	4–5 hrs
Starting Grid Reference:	424093
Grade:	Hillwalk 2
Map:	4
O.S. map 1:50,000:	70

16. The standard peak-bagging route on Brandon is the Saint's Road on the west side which starts at An Baile Brac (424093), and is signposted. It is tough, unrelenting and thoroughly rewarding for anybody who wishes to reach the top of one of Ireland's holy mountains. It is almost impossible to get lost, as the route first follows a track to a gate in a broken down wall, and then a mountain path by a stream along an old wall. The path is cairned in its upper section. The trig. station and the remains of Brendan's oratory can be found on the summit. Return the way you came, or head south along the easy ridge by the wall to Gearhane via Brandon Peak. From here, pass through the highest gate in Ireland, and down the ridge southwest, then west to Ballinloghlig, and back by road to An Baile Brac.

ROUTE 17

Mountain Group:	Brandon
Route Name:	The Pilgrim's Path
Distance from start to finish:	8km
Height Gain:	772m
Average time from start to finish:	4–5 hrs
Starting Grid Reference:	494119
Grade:	Hillwalk 3
Map:	4
O.S. map 1:50,000:	70

17. Brandon is a holy mountain and its main pilgrimage route is from the east. This is the quickest and most pleasant route on the mountain for the hillwalker. It starts at Faha (494119) where there is parking for about five cars. Alternatively, park at the church in Cloghane, and start from sea level. The path from Faha goes through a gate which is signposted, and the route is marked by red and white poles. The first thing you come across is a grotto erected as a memorial to various locals. Then it is off across the mountainside keeping under the ridge line, and gradually gaining the crest. You contour left on a good path, while those heading for the Faha ridge go straight on. The path undulates along the steep side of the glen, and rises until the poles come to a stop. They are replaced by paint with helpful signs like 'way

down' and arrows so it is almost impossible to get lost. At the back wall of the glen a good path leads in a zig zag up to the main Brandon ridge. At the top look down the valley you have come up, and the view is worth the climb. A sign in English and German (but not Irish) points the way down, but you should continue south on the path to the summit of Brandon mountain, about 80m above you.

ROUTE 18

Mountain Group:	Brandon
Route Name:	Lough Cruite Horseshoe
Distance from start to finish:	14.5km
Height Gain:	1174m
Average time from start to finish:	5.5–6.5 hrs
Starting Grid Reference:	491085
Grade:	Hillwalk 4
Map:	4
O.S. map 1:50,000:	70

18. An alternative start to the previous route provides the possibility of an excellent horseshoe walk on the east side of the mountain. Parking for two or three cars can be found at the bridge (491085) over the Owenmore stream coming out of Lough Cruite. Follow the boreen until you can exit onto the open mountainside. If you are in any doubt as to the route ask permission from the farmer. The route follows a broad ridge on the right side of the stream and the seemingly innocuous nature of the ground soon gives way to wild country as you turn the corner into the glen. You will have to cross a few sheep fences on this route, but you can ensure that no damage is done by following along to the right point before crossing. Follow the falls between Lough Cruite and Lough

Nalacken on the right side and the way appears barred by the falls at the back of Lough Nalacken. This is easily ascended on the left by a ramp, and the more adventurous can try their hand at the falls. The third fall can be passed on the right and from here the route joins with the Pilgrim's Path to take you up the back wall and on to the summit. Continue south as far as Gearhane and continue south beside the cliffs. Follow the fence down the long ridge before dropping down the little cliff to the road. You can also go down the east side of the Gearhane, but it is a lot harder on the ould knees!

ROUTE 19

Mountain Group:	Brandon
Route Name:	The Faha Ridge
Distance from start to finish:	8km
Height Gain:	875m
Average time from start to finish:	4–5 hrs
Starting Grid Reference:	494119
Grade:	Scramble 1 or 5
Map:	4
O.S. map 1:50,000:	70

19. The hardest ordinary route up Brandon is the Faha ridge and even though the difficult section is no more than a kilometre in length it is an excellent route. Begin at Faha as you would for the Pilgrim's Path (494119) and follow this until it joins the ridge line. A wall runs along the crest of the ridge. Follow the wall until it turns left, and into the coum. Continue up the hill to the summit which is also called Gearhane. The fun begins and you set off on the narrow crest up and down over the pinnacles until you reach the second summit. A track runs along the ridge in places, but the pinnacles are much more fun, even if a little exposed. Descend from this, and then you are invited to proceed along a long slab. The slab rises gradually, and ends in a straight drop to the end of the ridge. The 10m drop requires extremely delicate

work on slimey rock and I do not recommend it without a rope. Instead just before you start on the slab you can descend awkwardly to your right and follow the track around to the base of the 10m descent. The way ahead offers two alternatives. One is to rock climb out of the gap between difficult and severe standard (route dependant) but the rock is somewhat loose so take care. The exposure here is incredible so plan B brings you right on a faint track, and up the back wall on grass and some rock to the end of the route. From here go left to Brandon or right towards Masatiompain.

ROUTE 20

Mountain Group:	Brandon
Route Name:	Loch an Mhóráin
Distance from start to finish:	4km
Height Gain:	733m
Average time from start to finish:	2.5–3.5 hrs
Starting Grid Reference:	491085
Map:	4
Grade:	Scramble 2/3
O.S. map 1:50,000:	70

20. A completely neglected place is Loch an Mhóráin. Having taken the road south at Cloghane, park carefully off the road at the bridge over the Owenmore (491085), and follow the track on to the open mountain. This involves hopping across the Owenmore just to the left of the farmer's house so take care. Follow around to the back of the lake (478088) 152m, and either climb the waterfall or just to the left of it on to the level ground at 500m. Both routes offer lots of scrambling options and the nearer to the falls you get the harder the scrambling gets. Either pick your way from here gently up the back wall of the coum on to Gearhane which is interesting or head left up a little ridge on to the east ridge of Gearhane. Follow this to the summit. Great fun can be had on these routes, but they get very

slippery when wet. Then again where in Kerry doesn't! Descend via the east ridge or go over the mountains to Brandon.

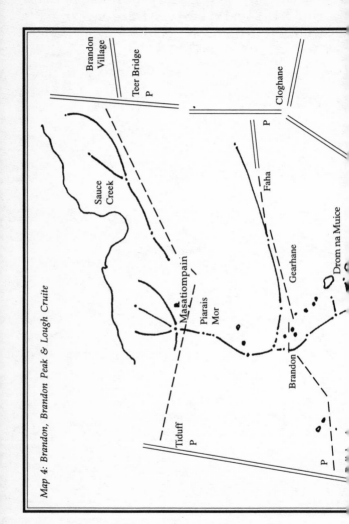

Map 4: Brandon, Brandon Peak & Lough Cruite

Brandon Village
Teer Bridge
P
Cloghane
P
Sauce Creek
Faha
Masatiompain
Piarais Mor
Gearhane
Drom na Muice
Brandon
Tiduff
P
P

50

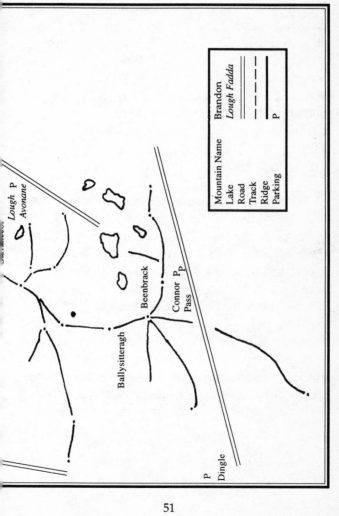

Lough
Avonane Lough P

Beenbrack

Ballysitteragh

Connor P P
Pass

P
Dingle

Mountain Name	Brandon
Lake	*Lough Fadda*
Road	
Track	- - -
Ridge	
Parking	P

51

Route 21

Mountain Group:	Brandon
Route Name:	Garranaceol
Distance from start to finish:	1–1.5km from lake
Height Gain:	640m
Average time from start to finish:	1.5 hrs from lake
Starting Grid Reference:	491850
Grade:	Scramble 1/2
Map:	4
O.S. map 1:50,000:	70

21. This is an easy scramble onto Brandon Peak, and can be used as an alternative to the Pilgrim's Path for those who know what they are about. Park at Faha and follow the path around the wood and down to the side of Lough Cruite. Follow a sheep trail halfway along the lake's left or west side to the base of Garranaceol (483097). A massive field of scree dominates the right hand face of the ridge. Our route follows the fall line and gradually levels off until it arrives on the summit of Brandon Peak. The route is not particularly difficult with just a few small rock steps but feels very exposed in places.

ROUTE 22

Mountain Group:	Brandon
Route Name:	Drom Na Muice
Distance from start to finish:	0.75km from lake
Height Gain:	640m
Average time from start to finish:	1–1.5 hrs from lake
Grade:	Scramble 2/3
Map:	4
O.S. map 1:50,000:	70

22. Instead of climbing Garranaceol continue up to the waterfall at the inflow to Lough Cruite (477104). At the top of these is a small area of level ground before you reach the outfall of Lough Nalacken. Drom na Muice ascends directly from here. The ridge begins steeply, and care should be taken especially on the wetter bits. The route keeps mainly to the skyline, and demands some traversing left or right of this. At about the halfway point the ridge levels off and it is an easy if narrow walk on to the main ridge. Off to your right is the even steeper Mystic Ridge, which starts from the inlet to the lake. This is a very severe rock climb, and so is outside the range of this guide. Contact the Dingle Mountaineering Club for information on this, and other Rock Climbing options in the area. Doonsheane just to the east of Dingle town even has its own guidebook.

ROUTE 23

Mountain Group:	Brandon
Route Name:	Owenafeana Horseshoe
Distance from start to finish:	16km
Height Gain:	1155m
Average time from start to finish:	6–7 hrs
Starting Grid Reference:	517139
Grade:	Hillwalk 4
Map:	4
O.S. map 1:50,000:	70

23. Park your car at Faha (494119) or alternatively at the school at Teer bridge (517139). If you park at Faha you will have a 180m walk back up to your car at the end of the day. From Teer bridge pass the school and take a track to your right. Head for the Faha ridge and follow this until the Faha path comes in on your left. Follow the path into the glen and climb the zig zags at the back wall. These will bring you to within 80m of the summit. Head south to the cairn, cross, well and gallán on the summit. From here head back north past the way down and continue along the main ridge towards Piarais Mor. The view of the Faha ridge from point 891m on the col to the north of it is glorious. Down to the col with its unusual sandstone tor in the middle. Skirt around this or climb it for the

fun and continue down to the stile for the Dingle Way. Off to your right is an Ogham stone which is worth a look, and after this continue on to the summit of Masatiompain. If you have no interest in Masatiompain then follow the markers east through the glen to the road about 100m from your car. If you climb Masatiompain follow the east ridge down to the old ruined village and then up to the rim of Sauce Creek which might be a coum drowned by the sea. From here drop down south to pick up the track that leads to your car.

ROUTE 24

Mountain Group:	Brandon
Route Name:	Lough Oughtragh Horseshoe
Distance from start to finish:	14km
Height Gain:	1030m
Average time from start to finish:	5.5–6.5 hrs
Starting Grid Reference:	431117
Map:	4
Grade:	Hillwalk 3
O.S. map 1:50,000:	70

24. Follow the signs for the Dingle Way on the western side of Masatiompan which lead from Ballinknockane (431117) and ascend an old track up the mountainside. As soon as you like, head over the boggy ground to Beennaman at 378m and follow the edge of the northern cliffs. These are spectacular. Either continue to the col to the south of Masatiompan and up to the summit or climb up the steeper west ridge to the summit. From here head south towards Brandon Mountain and enjoy the view down into the Paternosters of the east side. Descend via the Saints Road until it meets the wall on your right at around 500m. Cross this and have a look into the little coum of Lough Oughtragh before heading west over the flat ground to point 454m. Down then to

the track by the outfall of Lough Eightragh and to
the road where you parked your car.

Route 25

Mountain Group:	Brandon
Route Name:	Ballydavid Head
Distance from start to finish:	5km
Height Gain:	336m
Starting Grid Reference:	403109
Average time from start to finish:	2–3 hrs
Map:	
Grade:	Hillwalk 2
O.S. map 1:50,000:	70

25. Ballydavid Head provides one of the best views of the Three Sisters and is well worth a visit on an afternoon. Park at either Ballyroe (403109) or just up the road in Graffe (408113), and head off up on to the hillside to the north. Keep going up the steepening hill to the summit of Beenmore which is one of the more spectacular views out over north Kerry. From here you head down west to the col. The cliff here is almost vertical and the wind tends to whip over the col so be extremely careful. Head up from here to the shoulder and then to the summit of Ballydavid Head with its old signal tower. The view over Smerwick Harbour and the Three Sisters is magnificent. Head west to spot 186m and down to Ballydavid, then back along the road to Ballyroe.

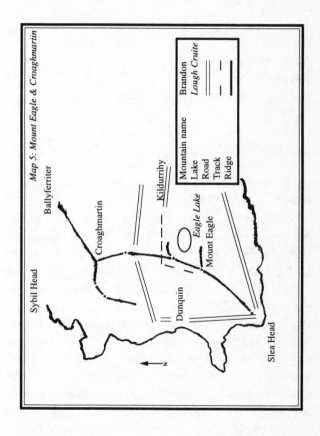

Map 5: *Mount Eagle & Croaghmartin*

Mountain name	Brandon
Lake	*Lough Cruite*
Road	
Track	
Ridge	

Sybil Head

Ballyferriter

Croaghmartin

Kildurrihy

Eagle Lake

Mount Eagle

Dunquin

Slea Head

N

ROUTE 26

Mountain Group:	Mount Eagle and the Blaskets
Route Name:	Sybil Head and The Three Sisters
Distance from start to finish:	5km/10km
Height Gain:	206m/400m
Average time from start to finish:	2–2.5/3.5 –4.5hrs
Starting Grid Reference:	320050
Map:	5
Grade:	Hillwalk 2
O.S. map 1:50,000:	70

26. Park at the Ostán Dún an Óir just beyond Ferriter's Cove (320050) and even if you did nothing more than sit in the bar, and watch the entire Atlantic break on the rocks of Doon it would be enough. From the Hotel follow the boreen north and up the track which leads to the old signal tower on the skyline. Head west from here to Sybil point. The view southwest towards Inishtooskert is one that appears on most calendars of Ireland, and is especially good on a clear November evening as the sun sets behind the island. Bring a camera and use a whole roll of film. From the point go east along the ridge and over a fence keeping to the ridgeline as much as possible. This can be rough enough when the wind is blowing.

After about 1.5km you can head south to pick up a track leading to Ballyoughteragh which will take you back to the Hotel via the Dingle Way or rudely across the golf course. However it is much more pleasant to continue up and over the Three Sisters which look very impressive from the ridgeline. From the summit of the last one head south along the coast to pick up a track which leads back to Smerwick village. It is a 5km walk back to your car along roads and then across the golf course to the Hotel.

ROUTE 27

Mountain Group:	Mount Eagle and the Blaskets
Route Name:	Mount Eagle
Distance from start to finish:	4km
Height Gain:	426m
Average time from start to finish:	2–3 hrs
Starting Grid Reference:	352002
Grade:	Hillwalk 1
Map:	5
O.S. map 1:50,000:	70

27. This is an afternoon stroll on easy ground on a rough track onto the north ridge of Mount Eagle. Start at Kildurrihy (352002) and head west past the television mast onto the ridge at 350m. From here head due south on the broad ridge keeping the cliff at your right. Descend southeast from the summit and the northeast towards your start point via Ballintea. So why bother with such a short walk? Two reasons: It is the farthest west hill in Europe, and, the view west over the Blaskets, south to Iveragh, east over Brandon and north to Ballyferriter is one of the best in all Ireland.

ROUTE 28

Mountain Group:	Mount Eagle and The Blaskets
Route Name:	Slea Head to Ballyferriter
Distance from start to finish:	11km
Height Gain:	869m
Average time from start to finish:	4–5 hrs
Starting Grid Reference:	352002
Map:	5
Grade:	Hillwalk 3
O.S. map 1:50,000:	70

28. While this walk will cause problems for the car driving brigade it is really too nice to ignore. Start at Slea Head (317967) which it is possible to get to by hitching a lift from some of the local tour buses. Start up the mountainside from the road along the ridge leading to Beenacouma. Continue from here up the broadening ridge to the summit of Mount Eagle at 516m. Continue north, keeping the cliff to your right until you hit the track coming up from the RTE mast. Keep going north over Coumaleague Hill and down to the col at Maumclassac (340015) where the Telecom mast is. Continue up Croaghmartin which is a bit of a slog to the 406m summit. From here head down the northeast ridge to the road just to the east of Bally-

ferriter. A pint in the Hotel is a good idea while you come up with suggestions as to how you are to get back to your car.

ROUTE 29

Mountain Group:	Mount Eagle and the Blaskets
Route Name:	Great Blasket Island Ridge
Distance from start to finish:	14km & 5km boat ride
Height Gain:	753m
Average time from start to finish:	5–6 hrs & 1 hr on boat
Grade:	Hillwalk 2
Map:	5
O.S. map 1:50,000:	70

29. It would be wrong not to include the Blaskets in a guide to Dingle even though to get to them is both difficult and expensive. The islands were abandoned in 1954 but not before a minor literary explosion produced a whole raft of books about island life. You must take a 'ferry' to the islands. Check in the Tourist Office in Dingle for information about boats out to the islands. The boats will land you on the Great Blasket and you should get one as early as possible to allow you complete the walk in time to get back to the mainland. In summertime you can stay on the island and boats from Dúnquin are no problem. Follow the old road out to Slievedonagh and where the track peters out continue to the summit. Follow the undulating

ridge to Croaghmore and on past the cloghan descending steeply to Ceann Dubh. Ahead of you lies America, Inisnabro, and Inishvickillane (home of former Irish Taoiseach, Charles Haughey). To the north is Inistookert which from the mainland looks like a body lying in the water. Return the way you came to get off the island.

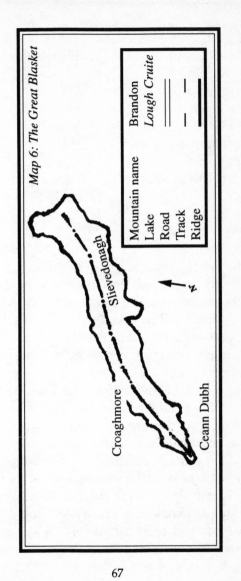

Map 6: The Great Blasket

Mountain name	Brandon
Lake	*Lough Cruite*
Road	
Track	
Ridge	

Croaghmore

Slievedonagh

Ceann Dubh

N

ROUTE 30

Mountain Group:	Sliabh Mish to Dingle
Route Name:	Peninsula Walk
Distance from start to finish:	65km
Height Gain:	3198m
Average time from start to finish:	22 hrs
Starting Grid Reference:	794118
Grade:	Hillwalk 5
Map:	1–4
O.S. map 1:50,000:	70/71

30. The whole peninsula can be followed along the top and is an excellent backpacking expedition. It usually takes three days at a good pace but can be completed in two if you wish. Park your car as you would for walk 6 and head off over the hills for Baurtregaum. From here head over to Caherconree and drop down to the Promontory fort for a look at the earthworks. Then go down south to the small col under Caherbla and then west to the road. Continue up over Knockbrack and northwest to the main Tralee/Dingle road. Stay at the old school hostel on the south side of Knockbeg which is a bit remote, but handy for the ridge. Climb up onto the ridge at Knockbeg and head for Knocknakilton. From here drop down to a large col and then up steeply to Dromavalla Mountain. Get out map 70. A line northwest will

bring you to the green road above Lough Anascaul and it is on over Windy Gap to Slievanea. Go west from the summit to pick up the track that will lead to the Connor Pass. On the other side of the Pass is Beenbrack and the easy ridge leads to Ballysitteragh with excellent views all the way along towards Castlegregory or Dingle. The ground falls steeply from Ballysitteragh to the col under Gearhane, and the pull up here is a bit of a slog. Continue along the level ridge to Brandon Peak and then drop down until you hit the wall that runs all along this section of the mountain. Just under the summit of Brandon Mountain leave the wall and follow the Saint's Road to the Cross and cairn. From here head north past the way down and continue along the main ridge towards Piarais Mor. The view of the Faha ridge from point 891m on the col to the north of it is glorious. Down to the col with its unusual sandstone tor in the middle. Skirt around this or climb it for the fun and continue down to the stile for the Dingle Way. Off to your right is an Ogham stone which is worth a look, and after this continue on to the summit of Masatiompain. Go east to Brandon Village or if you prefer Feoghnach on the west side for a swim, food and a pint. If you have no friends hitch a lift to Dingle and get the bus back to Tralee.